PLATE TECTONICS

Charlotte Luongo

This edition first published in 2010 in the United States
of America by Marshall Cavendish Benchmark.

Marshall Cavendish Benchmark
99 White Plains Road
Tarrytown, NY 10591
www.marshallcavendish.us

Library of Congress Cataloging-in-Publication Data
Luongo, Charlotte.
Plate tectonics / by Charlotte Luongo.
p. cm. — (Big ideas in science)
Summary: "Provides comprehensive information on the theory of plate tectonics
and how it affects our lives today"—Provided by publisher.
Includes bibliographical references and index.
ISBN 978-0-7614-4397-1
1. Plate tectonics—Juvenile literature. I. Title.
QE511.4.L86 2010
551.1'36—dc22
2009000130

The photographs in this book are used by permission and through the courtesy of:
Cover: Michael C. Gray/Shutterstock; Peter Zurek/ Shutterstock.
Half Title: NASA
p6: NASA; p7: Corbis; p8t: Dean Turner/iStockphoto; p8b: Karl Zemlin/iStockphoto;
p10: Bettmann/Corbis; p11: Hulton Archive/Getty Images; p13: Fine Art Photographic Library/
Corbis; p14: Shutterstock; p15: Jonathan Blair/Corbis; p16: John Cancalosi /Photolibrary;
p17: Walter Geiersperger/Corbis; p20: Cambridge University Press; p22: North Wind Picture
Archives; p23: Naval Historical Foundation; p24: U.S. Navy; p25: NOAA; p26: Joanna Vestey/
Corbis; p30-31: S. Jonasson/FLPA; p32: Department of Physics/University of Toronto; p33: GNS
Science Photolibrary; pp34-35: USGS; p36: Shutterstock; p37: USGS; p38: USGS;
p39: NGDC/NOAA; p43: Lockheed Martin Corporation; p44: ESA © 2007 MPS for OSIRIS Team
MPS/UPD/ LAM/IAA/ RSSD/ INTA/ UPM/ DASP/ IDA; p45: NGDC/NOAA.
Illustrations: Q2AMedia Art Bank

Created by Q2AMedia
Art Director: Sumit Charles
Editor: Denise Pangia
Series Editor: Penny Dowdy
Client Service Manager: Santosh Vasudevan
Project Manager: Shekhar Kapur
Designers: Shilpi Sarkar and Joita Das
Illustrators: Prachand Verma, Ajay Sharma,
Bibin Jose, Abhideep Jha, and Rajesh Das
Photo Research: Shreya Sharma

Printed in Malaysia

135642

Contents

Introduction

Take a look at this map of Earth. The position and shape of the **continents** are probably familiar to you. But Earth has not always looked like this.

In the past, the shape and position of the continents were very different. For example, look at South America and Africa. Did you know that these two continents were once joined together? They were part of the same landmass. But, millions of years ago, they broke apart.

How could a giant piece of land break apart? This can happen because the Earth's **crust** is made up of many pieces. These pieces move, causing the continents to move with them. This concept, or idea, is called plate tectonics.

Today, this idea may not seem very strange. In fact, you may have heard about it before. But when plate tectonics was first introduced, very few people believed that it could possibly be true. In fact, many laughed at it. Yet, plate tectonics was no joke. Over time, a large amount of evidence was found that supported it.

ARCTIC OCEAN

NORTH AMERICA

NORTH PACIFIC OCEAN

NORTH ATLANTIC OCEAN

SOUTH AMERICA

SOUTH PACIFIC OCEAN

SOUTH ATLANTIC OCEAN

Today, all of earth science is based on the idea of plate tectonics. Scientists use this idea to explain how mountains, cliffs, and many other features on Earth have formed. Plate tectonics also helps explain what causes earthquakes and volcanic eruptions.

You are about to find out about the story of how plate tectonics changed from fiction to fact. You'll also learn how the remarkable ideas of a few scientists changed how we look at our world.

ARCTIC OCEAN

EUROPE

ASIA

NORTH PACIFIC OCEAN

AFRICA

INDIAN OCEAN

AUSTRALIA

The Way the World Was

How old is Earth? At one time, most people thought it was only a few thousand years old. It was not until the nineteenth century that some scientists began to think Earth was far, far older than that. Their ideas became the focus of heated debate.

The study of Earth, its materials, and its physical history is called **geology**. Up until the 1800s, many geologists believed Earth was very young. They thought Earth's landforms, such as mountains and oceans, were formed by catastrophes, or sudden changes in Earth. Since these changes happened quickly, Earth didn't have to be very old to develop the features it did. These scientists believed that volcanoes, violent floods, and asteroids shaped Earth early in its life as a planet.

Just how old is Earth? Early scientists thought it was only a few thousand or perhaps a million years old. Earth, however, is more than four billion years old.

Through the early 1900s, geologists argued about how Earth's landforms were formed. Eventually, both sides realized they were wrong—and right! Today, geologists agree. Earth's features were formed through both slow and fast processes. Catastrophic events can cause large canyons and other features to form quickly. Yet, mountain chains and river deltas take millions of years to form. Plate tectonics is a very slow process. You are about to find out more about it. The movements it causes are very small. Over the course of a person's life, they can only be measured in centimeters.

Other geologists thought that Earth was very old. These scientists were called uniformitarians. They believed that all of Earth's features were made by slow, uniform processes. If this were true, it would have taken billions of years for Earth's landforms to develop. At the time, though, there was little evidence to support this claim.

One of the most famous scientists of the 1800s, William Thomson, tried to settle the debate. Because of some of his brilliant discoveries in physics, Thomson was given the title Lord Kelvin. Though not a geologist, Lord Kelvin believed that Earth's landforms were formed by catastrophes. He was determined to prove it. Thomson started with an idea that was common at

Lord Kelvin was a brilliant, confident scientist. He is best known for his work on a special kind of temperature scale. It is still used by modern physicists. It is known as the Kelvin temperature scale.

the time: Earth was once part of the Sun. At some point it had broken off and become a planet. Because of this, Earth had once been the same temperature as the Sun. Over time it had cooled down. So, Kelvin used known cooling rates to calculate Earth's age. According to him, Earth was only one hundred million years old.

Lord Kelvin's statement caused an uproar! If he was right, then uniformitarians were wrong. One hundred million years was not enough time for Earth's features to have formed slowly. Many geologists attacked Kelvin's calculation. They stated (correctly) that his ideas were probably wrong. Even if he wasn't a geologist, however, Lord Kelvin was a famous scientist. So, for years, many people believed him.

Scientists who believed Lord Kelvin's theory also **hypothesized** that as Earth cooled, it shrank. This caused ridges and valleys to form. Think of a rotting, shriveling tomato. As its skin contracts, it wrinkles. This idea of how some of Earth's features were formed stayed popular even after Lord Kelvin was proven wrong.

What caused Lord Kelvin to be proven wrong? It was a handful of salt—and not the kind of salt that you put on your food. It was uranium salt. The French scientist Antoine Henri Becquerel was studying uranium, which is a heavy metal. Becquerel realized that the metal was radioactive. Radioactivity is the process of a material giving off energy as it breaks down. This energy takes the form of heat.

In the late 1800s, most geologists thought early Earth was similar to this ripe tomato. They pictured early Earth as a smooth sphere of molten, or liquid, rock.

Geologists then hypothesized that as early Earth cooled, its surface shrank. This caused valleys and mountains to form. This process would have been similar to the one that caused the wrinkles on this dried-out tomato.

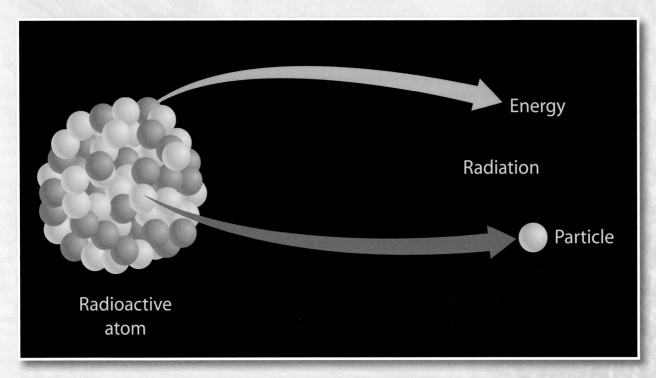

Energy

Radiation

Particle

Radioactive atom

Radioactive atoms give off energy in the form of heat. Earth's core is made of atoms such as this one. As they break down, their heat keeps the planet's temperature stable.

Scientists realized something after the discovery of radioactivity. If radioactivity gives off heat, then radioactive materials could keep Earth warm. This meant that Lord Kelvin's calculation of Earth's age must be false! Scientists also learned that radioactive materials break down into other materials. This information gave scientists a new tool. They could now calculate the age of a rock by measuring how much of the radioactive material in the rock had broken down. Scientists used this method to recalculate Earth's age. They found that the uniformitarians were right. Earth is very, very old. In fact, Earth is over four billion years old.

American scientist Bertram Borden Boltwood was the first person to discover radiometric dating, which is the use of radioactive materials to find out how old something is. In 1907 Boltwood was studying uranium. As uranium breaks down, it becomes lead. Uranium breaks down at a steady pace. Boltwood realized that you could measure the amount of lead in a uranium rock. Then you could find out how old the sample was. Today, scientists use this method to date many different things.

Alfred Wegener
A Scientific Revolutionary

The age of Earth was debated mainly among British geologists. These scientists studied mountains and collected the traces of ancient living things to support their arguments. Then, in 1880, Alfred Wegener was born in Germany. He would later propose a groundbreaking theory that would change how everyone thought about Earth and how it formed.

Wegener's father and grandfather were both ministers, but Alfred and his brother Kurt showed a strong interest in science. Wegener also had an explorer's spirit. He dreamed of going on an expedition to Greenland and the Arctic.

His adventurous spirit came in handy. In 1905 Wegener earned his doctoral degree in astronomy, or the study of bodies in space. However, he was also interested in meteorology, which is the study of Earth's weather. He began using hot air balloons to study weather and air circulation. In 1906, he and his brother set a world record by staying in the air for more than fifty-two hours!

The Wegener's hot air balloon ride was very dangerous. Hot air balloons were less stable than they are today. Also, they did not have oxygen tanks. This meant they had to be very careful not to travel up too high. This didn't seem to bother the brothers.

Alfred Wegener had an adventurous spirit.
He took part in many daring explorations.

While doing research for the Royal Prussian Aeronautical Observatory, Alfred Wegener and his brother Kurt also broke the world record for the longest hot air balloon flight.

While on their flight, they collected information about the weather. Both the flight and the information caught the attention of many people.

Wegener was soon invited to join an expedition to Greenland. He was delighted! Here was a chance to fulfill his boyhood dream. Wegener signed on as the group's meteorologist. While on the trip, he used his kites and balloons to study the atmosphere over the Arctic.

Wegener returned to Germany and was offered a teaching job. He taught both astronomy and meteorology classes. His students seemed to like his teaching style. Other teachers also liked him. They were impressed with his ideas about weather. Nobody would have dreamed that Wegener was about to become one of the most controversial figures in science.

All of Wegener's expeditions were dangerous. Some almost cost him his life. In 1912 a **glacier** in Greenland split in two. The group had to hike 750 miles (1,207 kilometers) on an ice sheet. They broke the record for the longest trek across an ice sheet.

Putting the Puzzle Together

Alfred Wegener turned thirty years old in 1910. That same year, a profound new idea began to form in his head. This idea would end up rocking the foundations of geology.

In 1910 Wegener was teaching about weather at the University of Marburg in Germany. One day, while looking at a world map, he noticed that the east coast of South America matched like a puzzle piece with the west coast of Africa! Wegener was not the first person to notice how well the continents fit together. Mapmakers had also noticed this. But Wegener quickly went beyond simply noticing the relationship. He came up with a hypothesis, or possible explanation, for why the shapes of the continents matched up. Was it possible, he wondered, that the continents had once been connected and later drifted apart?

The theory of continental drift is now a cornerstone of modern earth science. It first occurred to Wegener when he noticed the puzzle-like fit of North America, South America, and Africa.

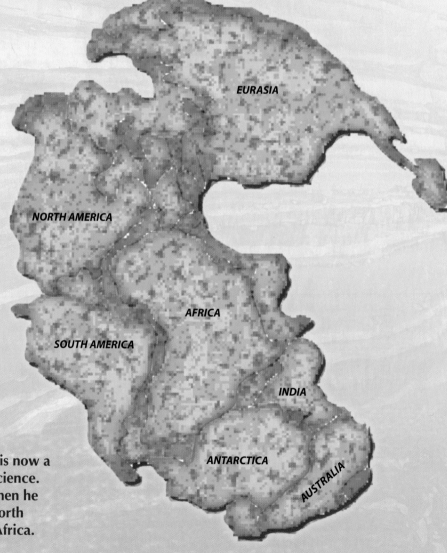

EURASIA

NORTH AMERICA

AFRICA

SOUTH AMERICA

INDIA

ANTARCTICA

AUSTRALIA

ORBIS TERRARUM NOVA ET ACCURATISSIMA TABULA. Auctore NICOLAO VISSCHER

The 1500s and 1600s are often called the Age of Exploration. Sailors circled the globe. They brought back information to mapmakers. As maps became more accurate, people started to notice that the coastlines of some continents seemed to match.

Wegener's idea, which was later called continental drift, is the theory that the continents move across Earth's surface, and have done so throughout history. Today this idea is accepted as fact. In Wegener's time, however, it caused an uproar. Many scientists called Wegener's idea absurd, and even dangerous.

Wegener did not limit his studies to the Earth. He also studied the crater formations on the Moon. Many scientists believed that the craters were the result of volcanic activity. Wegener instead believed they were a result of meteors hitting the surface of the Moon. His idea turned out to be correct.

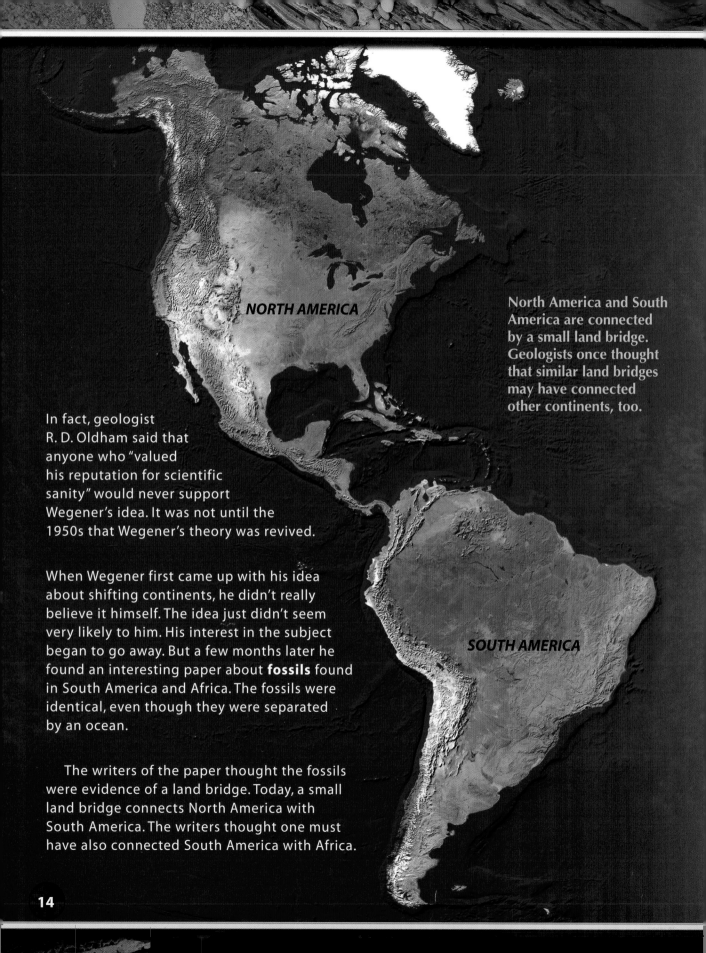

NORTH AMERICA

North America and South America are connected by a small land bridge. Geologists once thought that similar land bridges may have connected other continents, too.

In fact, geologist R. D. Oldham said that anyone who "valued his reputation for scientific sanity" would never support Wegener's idea. It was not until the 1950s that Wegener's theory was revived.

When Wegener first came up with his idea about shifting continents, he didn't really believe it himself. The idea just didn't seem very likely to him. His interest in the subject began to go away. But a few months later he found an interesting paper about **fossils** found in South America and Africa. The fossils were identical, even though they were separated by an ocean.

The writers of the paper thought the fossils were evidence of a land bridge. Today, a small land bridge connects North America with South America. The writers thought one must have also connected South America with Africa.

SOUTH AMERICA

A land bridge explained how the same plants and animals could have once lived on both continents. The writers thought that the land bridge either sank or washed away.

Wegener did not think the land bridge idea was right. The land bridge that connects North America and South America is very small. A land bridge connecting South America with Africa would have to be thousands of miles longer. Plus, there was not a single trace left of this land bridge. There were no chains of islands bridging the gap, and no parts of the Atlantic Ocean seemed strangely shallow.

But Wegener was sure of one thing: South America and Africa had been connected. He knew that the two continents had very different plants and animals, but the fossil record showed that, millions of years ago, the same plants and animals lived on both. How could this be? Wegener started to read more about fossils and found that there were many instances where identical fossils had been discovered on different continents.

Wegener also read about the rocks on each continent. Some of these rocks had scratches. The scratches were made by huge glaciers, which are ice sheets, that moved over the rocks about 300 million years ago. The scratches show the direction the glaciers moved. Wegener realized that the glaciers that had traveled over South America and Africa had moved in the exact same direction.

Wegener was intrigued by the fossils of a reptile called *Lystrosaurus*. Fossils of *Lystrosaurus* were found in Africa, Madagascar, Antarctica, and India.

15

In South America and Africa, *Mesosaurus* and *Glossopteris* fossils were found. A *Mesosaurus* is a kind of lizard that lived in bodies of fresh water. *Glossopteris* is a kind of plant that could only grow in warm, tropical places. These fossils were about 250 million years old. *Glossopteris*, in particular, interested Wegener. This was because fossils were found not only in South America and Africa, but also in Antarctica, India, and Australia. How could the same plant have grown on opposite sides of three oceans? Were all these continents once connected by land bridges? Wegener did not think so.

Also, how could a tropical plant have once grown in Antarctica? Today, Antarctica is very cold. It is almost entirely covered by ice. However, fossils of many tropical plants and animals were found in Antarctica. To Wegener,

The first version of Wegener's book *The Origin of Continents and Oceans* was only printed in German. It was only ninety-four pages long. Very few people read it. In 1919, Wegener added more evidence and included an index. When the third edition came out in 1922, it was even longer. Also, the publisher printed it in several different languages. This time, scientists from around the world took notice. They began to attack the book almost immediately.

Mesosaurus fossils are found in the southern parts of South America and Africa.

this meant one of two things. Either Earth's climate was once very different, or the continents were once in different places.

Other evidence supported the idea of continental drift. Fossils of clams were found on mountaintops. Proof of glaciers was found in the middle of hot deserts. Then Wegener read about similar rock layers being found on both sides of the Atlantic Ocean. Finally, he was convinced of his own theory. He concluded that more than 200 million years ago, the continents must have been connected. Over time they broke apart and moved across the globe. Climates changed according to the continents' new locations.

Fossils of *Glossopteris* helped convince Wegener that the continents were once found in different locations on Earth's surface.

Wegener started sharing his ideas about continental drift with a paper in 1912. Then he published all his ideas in 1915 in *The Origin of Continents and Oceans*. He was not prepared for the controversy it would cause.

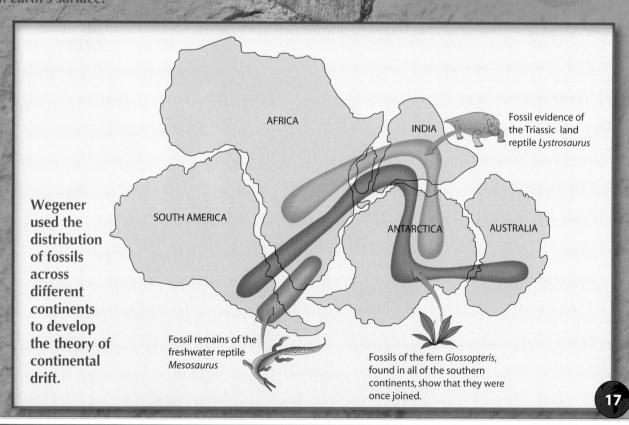

Wegener used the distribution of fossils across different continents to develop the theory of continental drift.

AFRICA

INDIA

Fossil evidence of the Triassic land reptile *Lystrosaurus*

SOUTH AMERICA

ANTARCTICA

AUSTRALIA

Fossil remains of the freshwater reptile *Mesosaurus*

Fossils of the fern *Glossopteris*, found in all of the southern continents, show that they were once joined.

17

A Very Dangerous Theory

Wegener's book *The Origin of Continents and Oceans* upset many geologists. Some called his ideas preposterous. Others said they were a fairy tale and even dangerous. These geologists thought Wegener's book was an attack on the very foundation of their science. They were right.

Wegener's ideas seemed crazy to most scientists, who believed the continents were fixed in one place. "If we are to believe in Wegener's hypothesis we must forget everything which has been learned in the last seventy years and start all over again," complained American geologist R. T. Chamberlin. This was why so many geologists did not like the drift theory. It changed everything.

Another reason geologists were skeptical had to do with Wegener himself. He was a meteorologist. What could he possibly know about geology? Critics questioned Wegener's credibility. They said he practiced bad science. Geophysicist Harold Jeffreys wrote that the drift idea was "a very dangerous one, and liable to lead to serious error."

Part of the problem with Wegener's drift theory was that he could not explain how it happened. Wegener knew this was a weakness in his argument.

Harold Jeffreys was one of many geologists upset by Wegener's book.

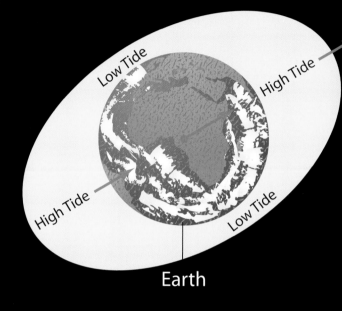

Direction of the Moon's gravitational pull

Moon

Low Tide

High Tide

High Tide

Low Tide

Earth

The Moon's gravity causes tides on Earth. Tides are the daily rising and falling of the ocean. Wegener did not know what caused the continents to move. He hypothesized that just as the Moon caused the oceans to move, it also caused the land to move.

He was sure that the continents moved. But what force could cause this? The continents were huge. Wegener suggested that maybe the Moon's **gravity** could drag the continents over time. He also thought that Earth spinning on its **axis** might have something to do with it. Maybe the spinning motion caused the continents to be pushed away from the **poles**.

Wegener knew neither of these ideas was very likely. He freely admitted that he did not know what caused the continents to move. This was the weakest part of his theory of continental drift. Other scientists used this weakness to attack Wegener's idea.

Wegener had a name for his idea that Earth's rotation, or spinning, caused continental drift: *polflucht*. *Polflucht* is German for "pole-fleeing forces." Every day, Earth makes one rotation around its axis. Because the axis runs from the North Pole to the South Pole, Earth's spinning motion causes winds to blow away from the poles. This fact led to Wegener's *polflucht* idea. However, Wegener considered the idea more of a suggestion than an explanation. He believed that the actual force moving the continents was yet to be discovered.

Jeffreys was one of Wegener's main critics. He did several calculations that proved gravity was not strong enough to move continents. He also proved that the spinning of Earth could not move a single rock, so it certainly could not move an entire continent. In 1924 Jeffreys published his book *The Earth: Its Origin, History and Physical Constitution*. This book seemed to mark the end of the drift theory. No serious geologist believed Wegener's idea. Geologists thought the drift theory was nothing but science fiction.

But Wegener did not give up on his theory. He continued to gather evidence, and he published updated editions of his book. Wegener also continued studying weather and tried to find a position teaching meteorology at a university. However, he was refused job after job. Universities thought that he was too interested in geology!

Harold Jeffreys's book *The Earth: Its Origin, History and Physical Constitution* seemed to prove Wegener's ideas wrong. The book was taught in geology classrooms for decades after its publication.

Wegener only reluctantly agreed to go on his last trip to Greenland. His group was supposed to deliver supplies to another research team. The team was spending the winter at a camp on the ice cap. Severe weather delayed Wegener's progress. Yet, Wegener would not give up. One of Wegener's closest friends was at the camp. He knew they badly needed the supplies. It took Wegener's group five weeks to reach the camp. Wegener wanted to return home. So, the very next day he set off again across the ice cap. He never finished the journey.

Even worse, he was not interested enough in his own field. Finally, in 1924, he was given a teaching job in Austria. A few years later, he was asked to go on another trip to Greenland. This would turn out to be his last. The weather was very cold. Temperatures dropped as low as −65°F (−54°C). Wegener tried to cross a huge ice cap in this weather, but did not survive the trek. His body was not recovered until the next summer.

Wegener died in 1930. The theory of continental drift all but died with him. Nine years after Wegener's death, Andrew Lawson was asked about the theory of continental drift. Lawson was a respected geologist. He answered, "I may be gullible. I may be gullible! But I am not gullible enough to swallow this poppycock."

Two more decades would pass before Wegener's ideas would be proven right.

Life of a Visionary

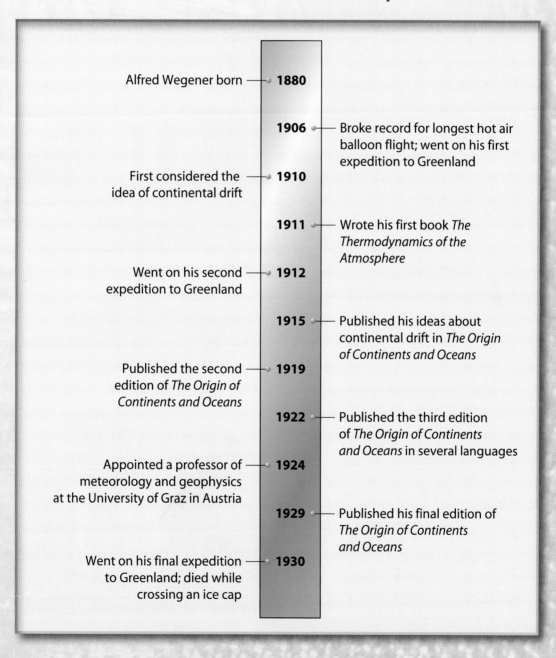

Alfred Wegener born — **1880**

1906 — Broke record for longest hot air balloon flight; went on his first expedition to Greenland

First considered the idea of continental drift — **1910**

1911 — Wrote his first book *The Thermodynamics of the Atmosphere*

Went on his second expedition to Greenland — **1912**

1915 — Published his ideas about continental drift in *The Origin of Continents and Oceans*

Published the second edition of *The Origin of Continents and Oceans* — **1919**

1922 — Published the third edition of *The Origin of Continents and Oceans* in several languages

Appointed a professor of meteorology and geophysics at the University of Graz in Austria — **1924**

1929 — Published his final edition of *The Origin of Continents and Oceans*

Went on his final expedition to Greenland; died while crossing an ice cap — **1930**

The Mid-Atlantic Ridge

Unfortunately for Wegener, proof of his theory of continental drift could not be found on land. It was far beneath the sea. In fact, it was about 3,000 miles (4,828 km) below the surface of the Atlantic Ocean.

The key to proving the drift theory was a chain of mountains underneath the Atlantic Ocean. The chain is called the **Mid-Atlantic Ridge**. It had only been discovered a few years before Alfred Wegener's birth. In the early 1800s most scientists thought the ocean floor was shaped like a bathtub. They believed the floor sloped down from the coasts and was very deep and flat in the center. This idea turned out to be wrong.

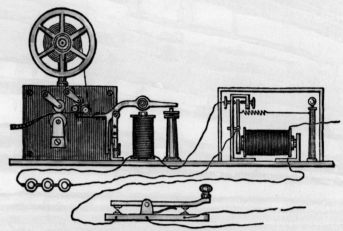

Morse apparatus, circuit, and battery

In the 1830s a new machine called the telegraph was invented by Samuel Morse. The telegraph used electricity to send messages through wires. Soon after the telegraph was invented, many miles of telegraph wires were set up. People could telegraph messages from one city to another. It was not long before people wanted to connect America to Europe with a telegraph wire that would cross the ocean. This would not be easy. People first needed to know more about the seafloor.

Morse key

These unusual items are pieces of the first usable telegraph. It was invented in 1835 by Samuel Morse. A few years later the U.S. Congress funded the laying of the first telegraph line. It ran from Washington, D.C., to Baltimore, Maryland.

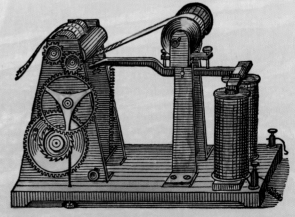

Morse register

The first transatlantic cable was made in 1857. It was 2,500 nautical miles (4,630 km) long and weighed 5,200 tons (4,717 metric tons). The cable snapped during the first two attempts to lay it on the ocean floor. In 1858 a third attempt was made. It worked! For the first time, messages could be sent from America to Europe within just a few minutes. However, within a few short weeks, the cable stopped working. The signal coming across the great distance was too weak to be read. It was Lord Kelvin who replaced the old instruments with newer ones that were able to read the weak signals.

In 1853 the U.S. Navy sent out a ship to explore the floor of the Atlantic Ocean. The ship was called the USS *Dolphin*. The technology used was very simple. The sailors tied a long rope around a heavy weight. Then they dropped the weight in the water and waited for it to hit the bottom. The sailors repeated this process about two hundred times all the way across the Atlantic Ocean.

The transatlantic cable was so large that it took two huge ships to carry it. During the first two attempts to lay the cable, large waves caused the cable to snap.

Lieutenant Matthew Maury was in charge of analyzing the navy's measurements of the ocean floor. Maury was surprised that the data showed a large bump in the middle of the Atlantic Ocean. He called the bump Middle Ground. A few years later the British Navy sent the HMS *Challenger* to take more measurements of the Atlantic Ocean's floor. The crew realized that the bump Maury called Middle Ground was actually part of a huge mountain chain that ran down the center of the entire Atlantic Ocean. Even more astonishing, the chain appeared to follow the curves of the continents on either side. The *Challenger* crew named the mountain chain the Mid-Atlantic Ridge.

The discoveries didn't stop there. Iceland is an island in the northern Atlantic Ocean. Scientists soon realized that Iceland was part of the Mid-Atlantic Ridge. The island was well-known for its volcanoes, which are places where melted rock comes up through Earth's crust. Iceland is not very large, yet it contains more than two hundred volcanoes.

Lieutenant Matthew Maury was the first person to realize that the ocean floor was not flat. He used the data collected by the crew of the USS *Dolphin* to make the first map of the ocean floor.

Then, in the 1920s, scientists began to study heat flow in ocean water. The studies showed that the water around the Mid-Atlantic Ridge was very warm. This showed that the Mid-Atlantic Ridge had many volcanoes. This fact would eventually help support Wegener's theory. Yet at the time, Wegener did not see any connection between those volcanoes and continental drift. No one did.

Iceland

— MID-ATLANTIC RIDGE

The Mid-Atlantic Ridge runs the entire length of the ocean floor. Notice how it mirrors the edges of the continents.

The crew of the HMS *Challenger* discovered the Mid-Atlantic Ridge. The crew was surprised to find huge mountains in the ridge. Some of them were a full mile (1.6 km) high.

The HMS *Challenger* set sail in 1872. Its mission was to collect as much information on the ocean as possible. The ship's staff included 240 scientists, sailors, and crewmen. The ship sailed around the world. Its trip took three years. Its crew measured how deep the ocean was. They took samples of the seafloor, too. Also, the crew discovered 4,717 new forms of sea life. In honor of the HMS *Challenger's* amazing journey, the National Aeronautics and Space Administration (NASA) named its second space shuttle *Challenger*.

H.M.S. CHALLENGER PREPARING TO SOUND, 1872.

Harry Hess and Seafloor Spreading

"Imagine millions of square miles of a tangled jumble of massive peaks, saw-toothed ridges, earthquake shattered cliffs, valleys, lava formations of every conceivable shape—that is the Mid-Ocean Ridge." —Maurice Ewing

Maurice Ewing was no sailor. He grew up on a Texas farm. He never even saw the beach until he was an adult. So, the last thing Ewing expected was to spend much of his life on a ship in the middle of the ocean. His long path to the sea started when he was sixteen and received a scholarship to Rice University in Houston. By 1931, at the age of twenty-five, he had earned his PhD in physics.

Ewing developed a new way to measure earthquakes. This interested geologists who were studying the ocean's floor. In 1934 Ewing was asked to participate in a mission to determine the structure of the **continental shelf**. This was the beginning of Ewing's life at sea.

Ewing collected information about the seafloor and related earthquake activity from oceans around the world. Eventually, he noticed a pattern in the measurements. Every ocean, it seemed, had a chain of

One of the scientists on Ewing's team was Marie Tharp. She discovered a large rift in the center of the Mid-Ocean Ridge.

mountains like the Mid-Atlantic Ridge. By 1956, Ewing and his team were able to show that the chains were all connected to one another. They measured approximately 40,000 miles (64,000 km).

One of Ewing's students gave a presentation in 1957. Harry Hess, a famous American geologist, was in the audience. When the presentation was over, Hess stood up and said, "Young man, you have shaken the foundations of geology!" At this point, Hess was only a few years away from giving his own foundation-shaking talks.

The mountain chains that run throughout Earth's oceans are known as the Mid-Ocean Ridge. The mountain ranges look like seams on a baseball.

In 1944 Ewing accepted a teaching position at Columbia University in New York. The team at Columbia wanted to learn as much as possible about the seafloor, so they took thousands of samples from it. These samples, called cores, were used to study the age of the ocean floor. They were also used to study what the floor was made of. Cores can be used to study past sea life, too. When Ewing started, only about one hundred seafloor cores had been collected. Ewing's team began collecting several hundred a year. Today, Columbia has about 19,000 cores in its collection.

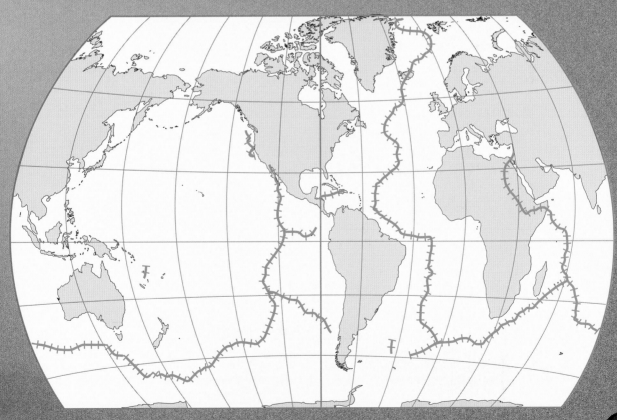

Ewing's research inspired Hess to begin studying the seafloor more closely. Hess read everything he could find on seafloors. Rock samples taken from the ocean showed a puzzling picture. None of the samples were older than 200 million years. This is far younger than the age of rocks on the continents. This discovery proved that the idea of a cooling, shrinking Earth was wrong. After all, if the Earth's crust had been formed all at the same time, the ocean floor would be as old as the land.

The next surprise came when the rock samples were mapped. The youngest rock samples came from the **Mid-Ocean Ridge**. The further away from the ridge a sample had been found, the older it was. This same pattern repeated itself in every ocean around the world. Hess also learned that the ocean crust is younger, thinner, and made of different kinds of rocks than the continental crust.

The ocean floor near the Mid-Ocean Ridge is very young. The farther from the ridge you get, the older the floor gets.

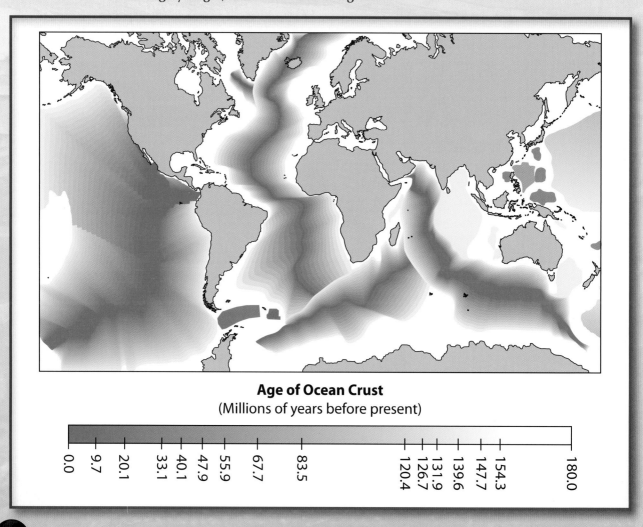

Age of Ocean Crust
(Millions of years before present)

0.0 9.7 20.1 33.1 40.1 47.9 55.9 67.7 83.5 120.4 126.7 131.9 139.6 147.7 154.3 180.0

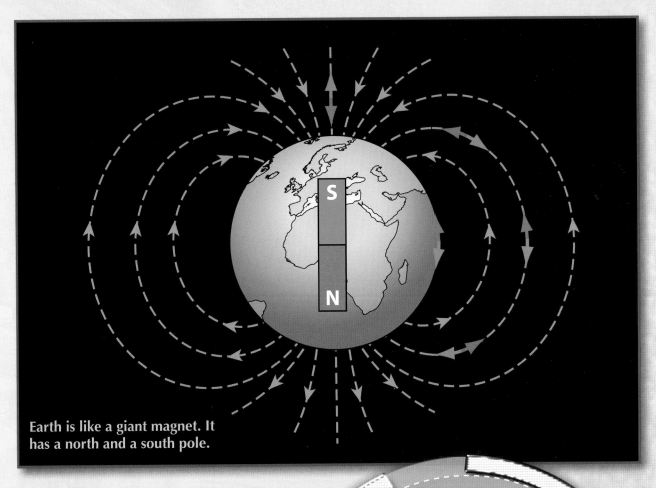

Earth is like a giant magnet. It has a north and a south pole.

The final piece of evidence that Hess looked at had to do with magnetism, which is a force between the poles of a magnet. Opposite poles attract. Like poles repel. Earth is like a giant magnet. It has a North Pole and a South Pole. Every so often, Earth's poles flip.

Many rocks have small bits of iron in them. Iron is magnetic. When these rocks form, the iron in them lines up with Earth's poles. Because of this, geologists can tell how Earth's poles were positioned when a layer of rock formed.

Harry Hess was a captain in the U.S. Navy during World War II. He was interested in the seafloor, so he decided to use his travels around the Pacific to do research. He used the ship's echo sounder equipment to do surveys of the ocean floor. To do an echo survey, sound waves are sent into the water. When the sound waves hit a solid object, they bounce off of it. This bounced-back sound, or echo, returns to the ship. The amount of time it takes for the echo to return determines how far away the object is. This information can be used to make a map of the seafloor.

In the early 1960s another study of the seafloor was done. Scientists looked at magnetic rocks on the floor. The results were surprising. Two hundred million years of Earth's history were recorded on the seafloor in a pattern of magnetic stripes. The stripes were parallel to the Mid-Ocean Ridge. On each side of the ridge, the stripes were mirror images of one another. Each stripe represented a time when Earth's poles had flipped.

Hess took one look at the images of magnetic stripes and knew what was happening. Volcanoes lined the Mid-Ocean Ridge around the world. Molten rock would rise up at the center of the ridge. When the molten rock met cool ocean water, the lava cooled and hardened. This explained why rock along the Mid-Ocean Ridge was younger than rock farther away from the ridge.

As more molten rock came up, it pushed aside the old rock. Slowly this caused the seafloor to spread apart. The spreading happened on each side of the Mid-Ocean Ridge. New rock came up, hardened, and then was pushed aside. This process had been happening for millions of years. It explained the record of magnetic stripes on each side of the ridge. It also finally explained what caused the continents to move.

Strangely enough, the force driving **seafloor spreading** had been first thought of two years before Wegener died. Scientist Arthur Holmes came up with the idea. He was sure that Earth was very hot underneath the surface. He thought that the layer of Earth under the crust was so hot that it flowed and moved almost like a boiling liquid. The material would rise and fall in huge circles. This created a current. Hess picked up on this idea. He used it to explain seafloor spreading. Hess thought that the moving material would drag Earth's crust along with it. The stage was set for the return of Wegener's continental drift theory.

About the same time Hess made his ideas public, a related event happened. On November 15, 1963, in the middle of the Atlantic Ocean, smoke, ash, and chunks of molten rock began bursting out of the sea. A new island was being born off the coast of Iceland. Scientists went to the Mid-Atlantic Ridge to watch the birth. The eruption continued for four years. Eventually the island grew to be 1 square mile (2.8 square kilometers). The island was named Surtsey. Today, ocean waves are slowly washing it away.

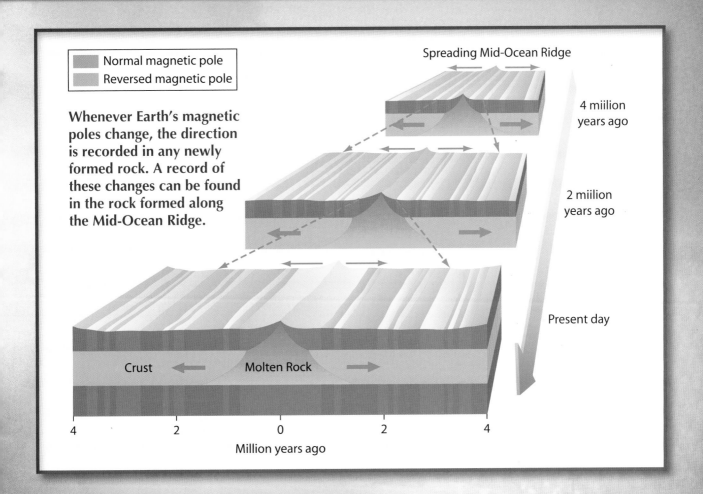

Normal magnetic pole
Reversed magnetic pole

Whenever Earth's magnetic poles change, the direction is recorded in any newly formed rock. A record of these changes can be found in the rock formed along the Mid-Ocean Ridge.

Spreading Mid-Ocean Ridge

4 miilion years ago

2 miilion years ago

Present day

Crust   Molten Rock

4   2   0   2   4

Million years ago

When molten rock emerges from a volcano along the Mid-Ocean Ridge, it hardens into new crust.

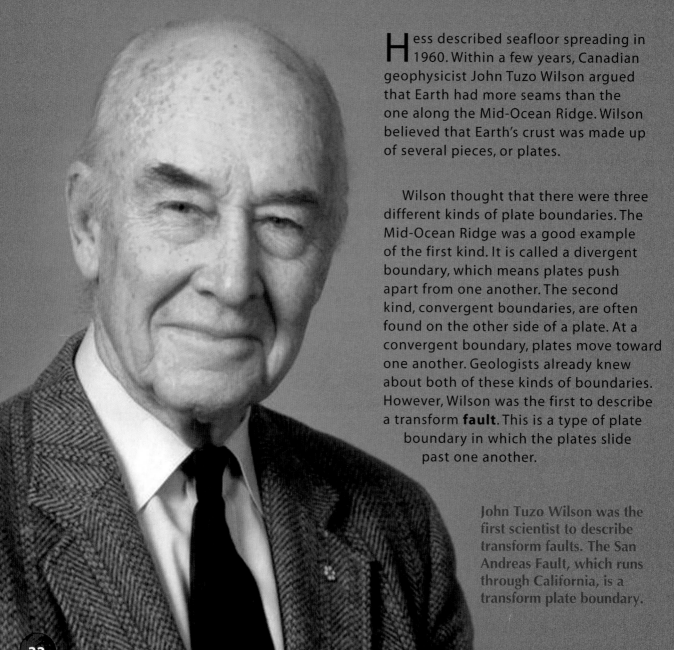

The Planet in Pieces

Harry Hess's discovery of seafloor spreading brought Wegener's ideas back to life. Almost overnight, geologists changed their view of Wegener. Wegener was no longer seen as misguided. Instead, he was praised.

Hess described seafloor spreading in 1960. Within a few years, Canadian geophysicist John Tuzo Wilson argued that Earth had more seams than the one along the Mid-Ocean Ridge. Wilson believed that Earth's crust was made up of several pieces, or plates.

Wilson thought that there were three different kinds of plate boundaries. The Mid-Ocean Ridge was a good example of the first kind. It is called a divergent boundary, which means plates push apart from one another. The second kind, convergent boundaries, are often found on the other side of a plate. At a convergent boundary, plates move toward one another. Geologists already knew about both of these kinds of boundaries. However, Wilson was the first to describe a transform **fault**. This is a type of plate boundary in which the plates slide past one another.

John Tuzo Wilson was the first scientist to describe transform faults. The San Andreas Fault, which runs through California, is a transform plate boundary.

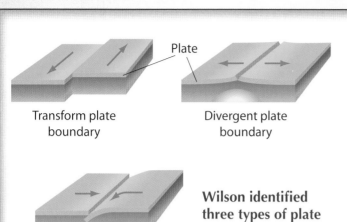

Transform plate boundary

Divergent plate boundary

Convergent plate boundary

Wilson identified three types of plate boundaries: divergent, convergent, and transform.

Plate

Wilson's ideas helped round out the continental drift theory. His ideas also gave rise to a broader theory called plate tectonics. The word *tectonics* comes from a Greek word meaning "to build." Plate tectonics has to do with the movement and growth of Earth's plates.

The long line you see in this picture is a plate boundary. The Australian Plate is on one side and the Pacific Plate is on the other.

John Tuzo Wilson once joked, "I enjoy, and always have enjoyed, disturbing scientists." Sure enough, many of Wilson's ideas have seemed a little strange to other scientists. But Wilson did not start out as a free thinker. He graduated from college the year Alfred Wegener died. At the time, he believed the shrinking and cooling theory about Earth. Wilson soon changed his mind. He started researching the continental drift theory and seafloor spreading. After that, Wilson became one of the main builders of the theory of plate tectonics.

According to the theory of plate tectonics, continents do not plow through the crust at the bottom of the oceans like Wegener had imagined. Instead, plates can push against, pull away from, and move past one another. As they move, some plates grow. Other plates get smaller. A plate can break apart and form two new plates. Likewise, two colliding plates can converge and become one.

Another scientist, W. Jason Morgan, added to the theory. In the 1960s geologists knew about several large faults around the world. A fault is a break in Earth's crust. Yet, scientists had no idea how these faults were connected. Morgan began reading everything he could find on faults. He soon found out that the faults could be followed for thousands of miles. They all seemed to be linked. Morgan thought that the faults were the borders of plates. Morgan guessed that Earth had about twelve major plates.

Scientists studied plate boundaries around the world. They soon noticed that most earthquakes occurred along the large faults that made up these boundaries. Most volcanoes were located there as well.

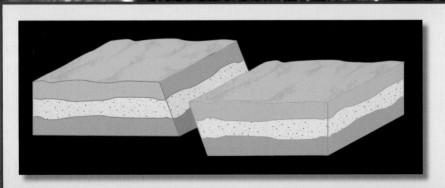

A fault is a break in Earth's crust. When pieces of crust move along a fault, an earthquake happens.

It began to appear that plate tectonics might explain a number of Earth's more dramatic events. There were still some unanswered questions, however. One had to do with the location of volcanoes. Some volcanoes were found in the center of a plate. How could these volcanoes be explained? As it turned out, John Tuzo Wilson had an answer.

The eruptions of Mount Saint Helens, a volcano in Washington, are caused by the movement of the Pacific Plate.

The border around the Pacific Plate is called the Ring of Fire, which gets its name from the many volcanoes along its edges. In fact, there are over 450 volcanoes in the Ring of Fire. They make up more than 75 percent of the world's volcanoes. Also, 90 percent of the world's earthquakes happen along the Ring of Fire. The ring makes a huge circle across the Pacific Ocean. The circle runs along the east coast of Asia and stretches down to New Zealand. It extends down the west coast of North and South America.

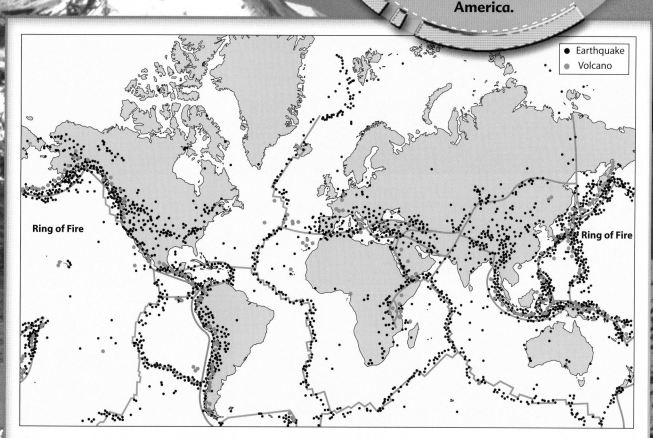

Ring of Fire

Ring of Fire

● Earthquake
● Volcano

This map shows the boundaries of Earth's tectonic plates. Compare the location of the boundaries with the locations of volcanoes and of earthquakes that occurred between 2003 and 2008.

Plates on the Move

Most of the world's volcanoes are found along the edges of plates. However, the Hawaiian Islands, which are a group of volcanoes, are found in the center of a plate.

John Tuzo Wilson found the Hawaiian Islands very interesting. The Hawaiian Islands are actually a string of volcanic mountains. The Hawaiian island chain runs west to east. The western islands are quiet. There are few, if any, eruptions there. The largest volcanoes are found on the eastern islands. In fact, Hawaii's most active volcano—Kilauea—is on the far eastern side of the eastern most island. Wilson wondered why this was the case.

Hawaii sits near the center of the Pacific Plate. Wilson imagined that the part of Earth underneath Hawaii must be very hot. He called this a **hot spot**. The hot spot heated the material above it. This material melted and became molten rock. The molten rock rose to the surface, causing a volcanic eruption.

Yellowstone National Park in Wyoming sits over hot spot. The hot spot heats groundwater. Sometimes the hot water explodes out of the ground. This causes geysers, such as the one shown here.

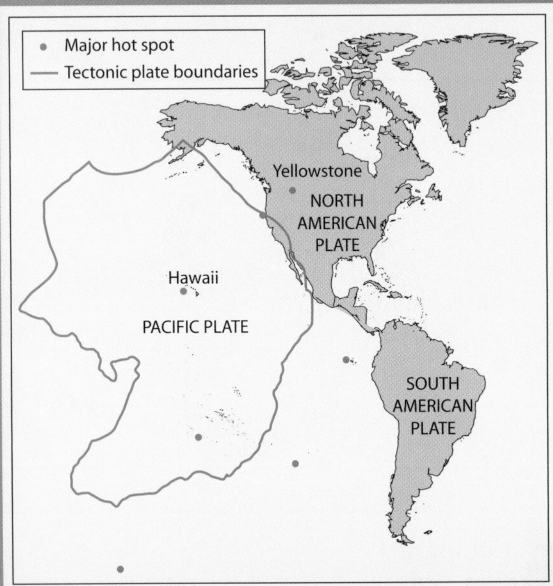

Major hot spot
Tectonic plate boundaries

Yellowstone

NORTH AMERICAN PLATE

Hawaii

PACIFIC PLATE

SOUTH AMERICAN PLATE

Hawaii is located in the center of the Pacific Plate. It is located over one of three known hot spots in the United States.

Lava, or molten rock, spills out of Kilauea, a volcano on the island of Hawaii. Hawaii is the youngest island in the Hawaiian island chain.

Wilson thought the hot spot must stay in the same place over time. However, the plate above the hot spot could continue to move. This explained how the Hawaiian Islands were formed. Over millions of years the hot spot caused a volcanic mountain to form. Yet, the plate that the mountain sat on kept moving. Eventually, the volcano stopped erupting. A new volcano formed over the hot spot. Soon, another volcanic island rose out of the sea. As the plate moved, yet another volcano would be formed. After millions of years the line of volcanoes would make up an island chain.

Island chains are very helpful to scientists. The chains give information about Earth's history. Island chains show which direction a plate has been moving. Also, rocks on each island can be dated. This tells scientists how old the islands are. Scientists can use this information to see how fast a plate moved. They can also use this information to determine what the Earth looked like millions of years ago.

	Continental crust	Ocean crust
Average age	3 billion years old	70–100 million years old
Average thickness	6 miles (10 km)	12–50 miles (20–80 km)
Most common rock	Granite	Basalt

Moving plates have created many other interesting landforms. One example is the Himalayas, one of the highest mountain ranges in the world. Most major landforms, such as mountain chains and deep valleys, are found along plate boundaries. The Mid-Ocean Ridge, for example, was formed along a divergent boundary, which means the plates push apart.

What forms along a convergent boundary depends on what kinds of crust—continental or oceanic—are moving into each other. The ocean crust is very different than the continental crust. Ocean crust is thinner and denser. What happens when continental crust collides with ocean crust? The thin, dense ocean crust sinks down underneath the continental crust.

The Himalayas, one of the highest mountain ranges, continue to get higher as the Indian Plate collides with the Eurasian Plate.

When one piece of crust sinks under another piece, a deep valley forms. This valley is known as a **trench**. As the ocean crust sinks, it becomes very hot and melts. The molten rock then rises up through the crust above it. This causes volcanoes to form. A very similar process occurs when two pieces of oceanic crust collide.

The process is different when two pieces of continental crust collide. As the pieces push against one another, they begin to buckle, or fold. The pieces thicken and the colliding plates are pushed up. This process causes mountains to form.

At a transform boundary, plates slide past one another. The edges of plates are not smooth. They are rough. Jagged pieces on the two opposing plates will catch against one another. This causes the plates to grind and jerk. The result is strong earthquakes.

The San Andreas Fault is found at the border of the North American Plate and the Pacific Plate. The two plates are sliding passed one another.

The San Andreas Fault is in California. It is a good example of a transform boundary. This fault forms the border between the North American Plate and the Pacific Plate. The North American Plate is slowly moving southeast, while the Pacific Plate is slowly moving northwest. This causes earthquakes along the west coast of the United States. If the plates continue to move like this, southern California will move up toward Alaska.

A Glimpse into the Past and Future

Alfred Wegener thought the continents were once joined together in one huge continent. He called this continent Pangaea. The name *Pangaea* comes from Greek words meaning "all land."

Giant continents like Pangaea are called supercontinents. Wegener thought Pangaea broke apart about 200 million years ago. Wegener was right. All of today's continents once formed a supercontinent about 225 million years ago. During this time the earliest dinosaurs lived on Earth.

It took millions of years for Pangaea to break into separate landmasses. When it first broke apart, North America, Europe, and Asia were part of land called Laurasia. Africa, Antarctica, Australia, India, and South America were part of Gondwanaland. Around 65 million years ago, the dinosaurs died out. By this time, Laurasia and Gondwanaland had split up into the continents you see today. However, they were not as spread out.

Two hundred million years may seem like a long time, but it's less than 5 percent of the entire time that Earth has existed. So, what came before Pangaea? Scientists think that the cycle of continents joining and breaking up has happened many times. In fact, there have been at least six giant continents formed in Earth's past. Scientists don't know exactly how this has happened, though. The continents may break apart and then move back together like a spring toy. Or the continents may break apart and move across the globe before colliding into one another again.

The supercontinent before Pangaea is called Rodinia, which comes from the Russian word for "mother." Scientists in the 1970s chose the name because they thought that Rodinia was the mother of all continents. However, geologists have since learned that there were other supercontinents before Rodinia. Rodinia existed from about 1.1 billion to 750 million years ago. The other supercontinents are still being debated. Scientists don't yet agree on how today's continents fit together to form these supercontinents. There is also debate over whether they were true supercontinents.

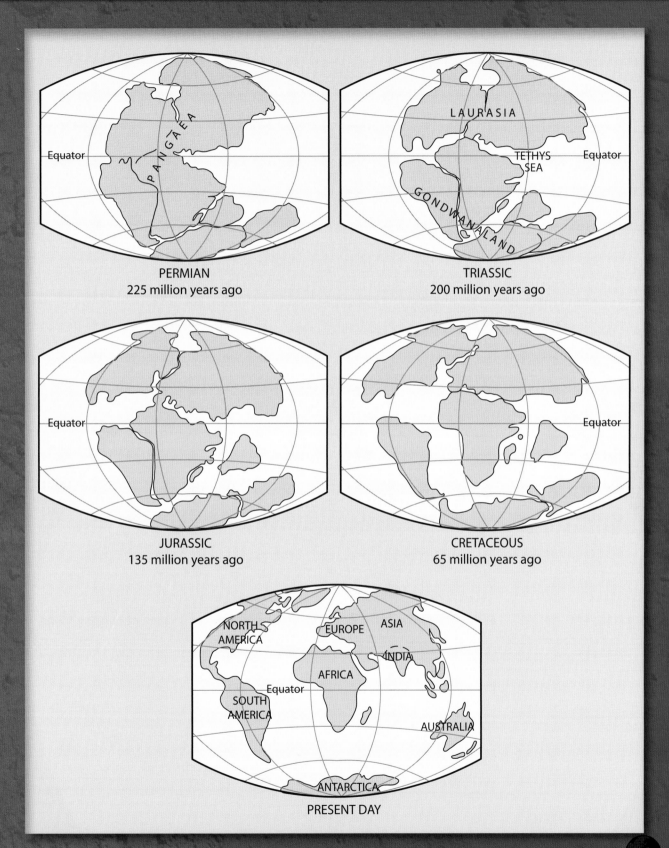

PERMIAN
225 million years ago

TRIASSIC
200 million years ago

JURASSIC
135 million years ago

CRETACEOUS
65 million years ago

PRESENT DAY

Where are Earth's plates headed next? Scientists aren't really sure. They are using satellites to help them find the answer. The satellites belong to the Global Positioning System (GPS). GPS satellites send radio signals to stations on the ground. Each station records the distance between itself and the satellite. As plates move, these distances change. Scientists use the data to see in what direction and how fast the plates are moving.

Plates move at different speeds. Some movement is steady. For example, the North American Plate is moving away from the Mid-Atlantic Ridge. It moves about 0.4 to 0.8 inches (1 to 2 centimeters) per year.

The Eurasian Plate, shown in the map below, is also moving away from the Mid-Atlantic Ridge. It moves at about the same rate as the North American Plate. So, the Atlantic Ocean is growing about 0.8 to 1.6 inches (2 to 4 cm) wider each year.

Some plate movement is not steady. For example, movement along transform boundaries is often jerky. The plates on each side of the San Andreas Fault might not move at all for several years. During this time, pressure is building up between the plates. When the two plates finally do move, they may jump 4 inches (10 cm) or more at a time.

This map shows the current direction of movement along different plate boundaries.

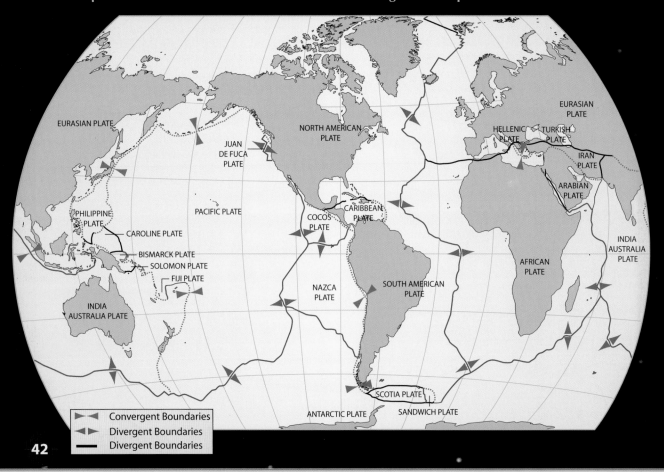

San Francisco was hit by a severe earthquake in 1906. During the quake, the plates along the fault moved several feet. In fact, one road crossing the fault was completely torn in two. In that area, land on each side of the fault was offset by 20 feet (6 m).

Scientists use satellites, such as this one, to track the movements of Earth's plates.

GPS satellites were not the first satellites used to study Earth's plates. Back in the 1970s, NASA put two satellites into space. They were called LAGEOS I and LAGEOS II. The satellites used lasers to measure changes on Earth's surface. This helped scientists study plate movements. It also helped them study Earth's rotation around its axis. The data showed that Earth wobbles as it spins. This is similar to a spinning top.

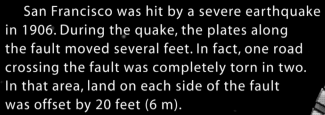

Unanswered Questions About Plate Tectonics

Today, the theory of plate tectonics is widely accepted. It is the base of the science of geology. However, there are still many unanswered questions. People are still searching for details. They want to know how the whole process works.

We still do not fully understand what causes tectonic plates to move. Early on, scientists thought that molten rock rising up pushed the plates. Now, scientists think that the opposite is most likely true. At some plate boundaries, oceanic crust sinks. It is the pull of this sinking crust that causes the plates to move. Yet, many scientists think that this may not be the whole story.

Scientists are still debating exactly how many plates Earth has. The most accepted estimate is twenty plates. Scientists are also trying to learn what affects a plate's size. Calculations show that plates should be no more than about 1,864 miles (3,000 km) wide, but the Pacific Plate is four times that size. Geologists are not sure why.

Scientists wonder whether other planets have plates. There is evidence that Mars (*left*) did in the past.

The movements of tectonic plates cause earthquakes. Strong earthquakes can destroy buildings and roads.

Geologists also want to know whether other planets have moving plates. As far as they can tell, Earth is the only one. What does this say about Earth? There is evidence that Mars had plates in the past. If this is the case, what happened to them?

Geologists ask these questions and many more. They want to learn more about our planet. Knowing how plates move is useful. Geologists hope they will one day be able to predict earthquakes and volcanic eruptions. This information could be used to make cities safe and to save lives.

Most scientists think that Mars had moving plates at one time. The first evidence supporting this idea was found in 1999. This is when Mars Global Surveyor spacecraft took several images of Mars's surface. The images showed magnetic stripes similar to those on Earth's ocean floor. This shows that, like on Earth, molten rock rose up to the surface of Mars. Plates were likely pushed apart. However, the surface of Mars does not move today. Scientists suspect the plates stopped moving millions of years ago.

Glossary

axis An imaginary line that an object spins around.

continent One of the main landmasses on Earth.

continental shelf The relatively shallow ocean plain that borders all the continents before sloping toward the ocean floor.

crust Earth's rocky outer layer.

fault A break, or fracture, in Earth's crust. Earthquakes often occur along fault lines.

fossil The trace or remains of an ancient living thing.

geology The study of Earth; earth science.

glacier A large, flowing sheet of ice.

gravity A force of attraction between objects that have mass.

hot spot A very hot area beneath Earth's crust.

hypothesize To state a possible explanation.

Mid-Atlantic Ridge The chain of mountains running down the middle of the Atlantic Ocean.

Mid-Ocean Ridge The chain of mountains running through all of Earth's oceans.

pole One of the two places on Earth's surface where the axis is located.

seafloor spreading The process by which new crust is created along the seafloor, causing it to spread.

trench A deep valley formed where one tectonic plate sinks beneath another.

Find Out More

Books

Arden, Carolyn. *Mountains and Valleys*. New York: Chelsea House Publications, 2009.

This book provides lively, descriptive explanations of how mountains form through the process of plate tectonics.

Stewart, Melissa. *Earthquakes and Volcanoes*. New York: Harper Collins, 2008.

This book, written in partnership with the Smithsonian Institute, is filled with fabulous illustrations.

Websites

http://www.howstuffworks.com/search.php?terms=plate+tectonics
This website offers multiple articles that explore concepts such as plate tectonics, Pangaea, seafloor spread, earthquakes, and volcanoes.

http://www.sio.ucsd.edu/voyager/earth_puzzle/
The Scripps Institution of Oceanography offers an interactive website that explores how Earth's plates move.

Index